It's Laugh O'Clock
Would You Rather?
Halloween Edition

Funny Scenarios, Wacky
Choices and Hilarious Situations
For Kids and Family

With Fun Illustrations

Riddleland

Designs by Freepik.com

www.riddlelandforkids.comcom

ISBN: 978-1-951592-91-2

TABLE OF CONTENTS

Riddleland Bonus

Join our **Facebook Group** at **Riddleland for Kids**
to get daily jokes and riddles.

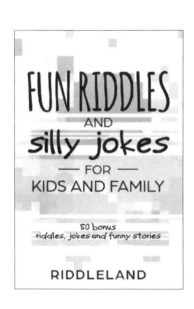

https://pixelfy.me/riddlelandbonus

Thank you for buying this book. As a token of our appreciation,
we would like to offer a special bonus—a collection of
50 original jokes, riddles, and funny stories.

INTRODUCTION

"It's as much fun to scare as to be scared."

~ Vincent Price

Are you ready to make some decisions? **It's Laugh O'Clock - Would You Rather? Halloween Edition** is a collection of funny scenarios, wacky choices, and hilarious situations which offer alternative endings for kids and adults to choose between.

These questions are an excellent way to get a fun and exciting conversation started. Also, by asking "Why?" after a "Would you Rather . . . " question, you can learn a lot about the person, including their values and their thinking process.

We wrote this book because we want children to be encouraged to read more, think, and grow. As parents, we know that when children play games, they are being educated while having so much fun that they don't even realize they're learning and developing valuable life skills. "Would you Rather . . . " is one of our favorite games to play as a family. Some of the 'would you rather ...' scenarios have had us in fits of giggles, others have generated reactions such as: "Eeeeeuuugh, that's gross!" and yet others really make us think, reflect and consider our own decisions.

Besides having fun, playing these questions have other benefits such as:

Enhancing Communication – This game helps children to interact, read aloud, and listen to others. It's a fun way for parents to get their children interacting with them without a formal, awkward conversation. The game can also help to get to know someone better and learn about their likes, dislikes, and values.

Building Confidence - The game encourages children to get used to pronouncing vocabulary, asking questions, and overcoming shyness.

Developing Critical Thinking – It helps children to defend and justify the rationale for their choices and can generate discussions and debates. Parents playing this game with young children can give them prompting questions about their answers to help them reach logical and sensible decisions.

Improving Vocabulary – Children will be introduced to new words in the questions, and the context of them will help them remember the words because the game is fun.

Encouraging Equality and Diversity – Considering other people's answers, even if they differ from your own, is important for respect, equality, diversity, tolerance, acceptance, and inclusivity. Some questions may get children to think outside the box and move beyond stereotypes associated with gender.

Would You Rather?
Halloween Edition

How do you play?

At least two players are needed to play this game. Face your opponent and decide who is **Pumpkin 1** and **Pumpkin 2**. If you have 3 or 4 players, you can decide which players belong to **Pumpkin Group 1** and **Pumpkin Group 2**. The goal of the game is to score points by making the other players laugh. The first player to a score of 10 points is the **Champion**.

What are the rules?

Pumpkin 1 starts first. Read the questions aloud and choose an answer. The same player will then explain why they chose the answer in the silliest and wackiest way possible. If the reason makes the Pumpkin 2 laugh, then Pumpkin 1 scores a funny point. Take turns going back and forth and write down the score.

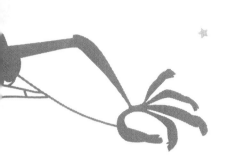

If you have three or four players

Flip a coin. The Pumpkin that guesses it correctly starts first.

> ### Bonus Tip:
> Making funny voices, silly dance moves or wacky facial expression will make your opponent laugh!

Most Importantly:

Remember to have fun and enjoy the game!

Dress up as a werewolf with curlers in its fur

as a ninja with fluffy pink bunny slippers?

Dress up as a dog and have to eat your food
out of a dog's food bowl

dress up like a ghost and have to roam the
cemetery all night long?

Would You Rather...

Dress up as an alien with a giant brain that makes you super smart but very unbalanced

dress up as an alien with a tiny brain but lots of arms and legs so you can move very fast?

Turn invisible on Halloween night so you can sneak as much candy as you want

lose your voice on Halloween and not be able to say "Trick-or-Treat"?

Have the head of a hard and empty bony white skeleton

the legs of a bloody brainless zombie?

Be able to make your skin disappear so you can be a skeleton for Halloween

be a real-life alien who can only show your true alien self on Halloween night each year?

Wear a facemask that makes your face all red, hot, and sweaty

wear a costume that is super itchy and uncomfortable?

Have a magic wand that shoots gobs of colorful bubbles into the air

sprinkles yellow, orange, and white candy corns every time you cast a spell?

Would You Rather...

Wear face paint that won't wash off for
a whole week

put a big curly gray grandma wig on your head that
won't come off for a month?

Fly a broom that needs to be filled with gas
at a gas station

that only flies if you chant "boo-chakka-boo"
the whole time you ride it?

Would You Rather...

Enter a school costume contest wearing a mummy costume made from soggy toilet paper wrappings

wearing a giant inflatable tyrannosaurus rex costume that everyone thinks is a cute puppy?

Be covered from head to toe with candied apple caramel

have a body like a snowman made from sticky popcorn balls?

Would You Rather...

Have bright pink bubblegum hair that everyone keeps trying to take a bite from

a chocolate bar bottom that leaves brown smears wherever you sit?

Dress as a scary beast that makes people laugh every time they see you

dress as a silly clown that makes people scream every time they see you?

Wear a ghost costume with no eye holes
so you can't see anything

no armholes so you can't carry a trick-or-treat bag?

Go trick-or-treating on Halloween when everyone
is wearing the same exact costume

go trick-or-treating on Halloween when no one
at all is wearing a costume?

Would You Rather...

Play hide and seek with the invisible man

play hide and seek with a blind mummy?

Pick any costume you want for your best friend
to wear trick-or-treating

have your friend get to pick any costume for you
to wear trick-or-treating?

Would You Rather...

Have a face that turns as orange as
a jack-o-lantern when you get embarrassed

smell like the inside of a rotten pumpkin every time
you start sweating?

Be able to take your eyeballs out of your head and use
them to spy on people

be able to take your ears off your head and use them
to eavesdrop on people?

18

would you Rather...

Be able to release your body heat through fiery dragon's breath so you never have to sweat

never get cold because you can wear the suit of an abominable snowman?

Have green scaly skin like a lizard

really hot smelly monster breath?

Have the power to raise the dead and bring someone who has died back to life

have the power to travel through time to visit any year you want?

Have eyes that randomly fall out of your head and have to be shoved back in your face

have a stomach with hands that randomly snatch food off of your plate at mealtimes?

Wear a monster mask so ugly that you can't look
at yourself in the mirror

be dressed up so beautifully that every time you
move sparkles fly off of your body?

Have skin that is pale and milky white
like Dracula

have hair growing all over your body like
a werewolf?

Be a witch whose only magical power is to turn everyone into toads

be a toad and try to convince someone to kiss you to turn you back into a human?

Live in a magical land where everyone but you has magical powers

live on earth with magical powers but you are never allowed to use them?

Have the power to turn dirt and earthworms into delicious chocolate candy bars

have the power to shoot candy corns from your fingertips like darts?

Only be able to say "I want to drink your blood" like Dracula on Halloween

howl and growl loudly like a werewolf on Halloween?

Wear face paint that smells like dirty socks

wear a face mask that smells like moldy cheese?

Go trick-or-treating wearing a baby carrier
on your chest with a baby doll that cries and wets

dress up as a baby and have to go to the bathroom
in your diaper?

Would You Rather...

Dress up as a witch with a hat that is too big and keeps falling over your eyes and blinding you

dress up as a mummy with wrappings that are too tight and your body goes tingly?

Have poisonous snake fangs that turn your victim's skin black and crusty

poisonous spider fangs that paralyze your victim so you can wrap them with a spider web?

Would You Rather...

Turn into a brainless zombie and forget how to read and write

have your teacher turn into a brainless zombie who can only stumble around and growl creepily?

Wear a Halloween costume that is made by your mom for trick-or-treating

go trick-or-treating dressed as your dad?

Would you Rather...

Be a wizard who can cast tons of spells but never be able to undo them

be a wizard with magical powers that are always glitching and doing unexpected things?

Have the power of super strength which is weakened whenever you eat a piece of candy

have the power of super stink which is strengthened whenever you eat a piece of candy?

Would You Rather...

Dress up in a superhero costume that requires you to wear your own underpants on top of leggings

have to dress up like a baby, including wearing a real diaper?

Turn invisible on Halloween night so you can sneak as much candy as you want

lose your voice on Halloween and not be able to say "Trick-or-Treat"?

Turn into a werewolf that yips like a puppy

transform into a vampire that can only
drink cow's milk?

Grow big hairy feet with long claws like a werewolf
so you can never wear shoes again

grow big hairy hands with long claws like a werewolf
so it's very tricky to go to the bathroom?

Would You Rather...

Wear a superhero costume with big inflatable muscles that won't stay blown up

wear a superhero cape that keeps flipping over your head and covering up your eyes?

Be a ninja who can't sneak up on anyone

get shrunk to one fourth of your size and spend your night dodging trick-or-treaters' feet?

Dress up with your friend as a horse and you have
to be the horse's butt

dress up as a cowboy or cowgirl and have to wear
boots with horse poo on them?

Have amazing superpowers that only work when you are
in the same room as your little brother or sister

be able to read your mom and dad's minds whenever
you want?

Would You Rather...

Be a really ugly wart-covered witch who can
do amazing spells

be a really beautiful witch who has
no magical powers at all?

Fall asleep in your costume and soak your bed with
sweat while you sleep

find a werewolf snuggled up next to you when
you wake up?

Would You Rather...

Be able to shoot laser beams from your eyes that instantly vaporize your homework

have a robot that lives in your stomach and calculates all the right answers for your homework, speaking to you through your belly button?

Have eyes that are clear blue when you are happy and change to bright red when you are angry

have a nose that grows long every time that you tell a lie and shrinks when you apologize?

Dress as a mummy with hot pink wrappings
that smell like roses

as a princess zombie wearing a sparkly crown and
a sash that says Ms. Undead?

Have skin that is made of rubber, so you are constantly
bouncing off things

have skin that is sticky like bubble gum, so you are
constantly getting stuck to things?

See everything through the eight eyes of a spider

crawl around for a day with the eight hairy
and sensitive legs of a spider?

Wear a mask that gets stuck on your face and has
no mouth hole so you can't eat any candy

wear a mask that makes sweat run into your eyes
so you can't see anything?

Dress as your P.E. teacher and keep yelling
at everyone to "drop and give me 10 pushups!"

dress as your music teacher who only speaks
in song?

Be a witch who can brew a magical potion for anything,
but you can't drink your own potions

have a wizarding little brother or sister who is always
casting crazy spells on you?

Turn into a skeleton whose bones rattle together
whenever you move

become invisible, but you have to stay naked
to stay invisible?

Grow long spiky cactus thorns all over your whole body,
so you have to cover yourself in pillows
for everyone's safety

have eye boogers that smell like rotting garbage leaking
out of your eyes?

Would You Rather...

Dress as an evil pirate with a parrot that keeps
pooping on your shoulder

as a beautiful long-haired princess whose hair keeps
getting tangled on everything?

Forget your Halloween costume at home on the day
of the school Halloween party and be the only kid
without a costume

end up wearing the same costume as four other
kids in your class?

Dress in a costume made out of cardboard and get caught in the rain so it gets really heavy and soggy

wear a costume made of duct tape that rips off your skin when you try to remove it?

Go trick-or-treating with your parents and get all your favorite candy

go trick-or-treating with your friends and only get candy you don't like?

Grow thick fur on your chest like a werewolf

have really dry papery skin that cracks like a mummy's?

Be chased by a scary clown while trick-or-treating

start crying "I want my Mommy" while going through a haunted house with your friends?

Turn into the tooth fairy and have to collect kids' gross bloody teeth every night all night long

 OR

turn into a fairy godmother that has to grant bratty princess wishes all the time?

Have your house's doorbell scream at trick-or-treaters when they push it

 OR

have a front door that drips with blood?

Would You Rather...

Be able to grow your hair as long as you want
when you say the magic word

have hair growing out of your nose that gets longer
every day even when you trim it?

Trick-or-treat only at creaky abandoned looking houses
on Halloween and get really awesome candy

trick-or-treat at normal looking houses but get really
yucky candy all night long?

Would You Rather...

Dress up as a ghost wearing a sheet that smells like dead fish

wear a witch's hat that smells like it's been sitting in her cat's litter box?

Try to eat your Halloween candy while bouncing in a jumpy house

try to eat a caramel apple while riding on a really bumpy school bus?

Would You Rather...

Be covered from head to toe in bird feathers
but unable to fly

eat all your meals by digging up earthworms
with your bird beak?

Have to brush your teeth after every single
piece of candy you eat on Halloween

have major toothache for one week after Halloween
because of all the candy you ate?

44

Would You Rather...

Wear clothes that smell like they've been stolen from a rotting zombie

wear a super sparkly glitter-covered full-length princess' gown?

Work at a school desk made entirely of chocolate that melts very easily

write with pencils that always have erasers made from bubble gum so you can never erase anything?

Would You Rather...

Be dressed as a Frankenstein monster with a mermaid's tail, baby doll's hair, the tentacles of an octopus, and a pirate's hook

be a zombie that can't die but everyone keeps trying to kill all night?

Have trick-or-treating at 6 o'clock in the morning on Halloween

have to go to bed at 6 o'clock at night on Halloween?

Would You Rather...

Be turned into a big hairy monster that looks really scary but is the kindest monster in the world

be turned into a cute and fluffy little monster who is the meanest monster in the world?

Eat mushy dog food flavored chocolate bars

lick a bunch of lollipops with your tongue turned sandpapery like a cat's?

47

Would You Rather...

Step on a melted chocolate bar with your bare feet

hold a chocolate bar in your hands until it melts and squishes through your fingers?

Get a bunch of Halloween candy that is in the wrong wrapper and doesn't taste like it should

have a bunch of candy that is wrapped in more than one wrapper and takes a long time to unwrap before eating?

Would You Rather...

Have to trick-or-treat walking backwards
in high-heeled shoes

trick-or-treat wearing rollerblades without brakes
in a hilly neighborhood?

Sit in a tree in your front yard all night in a ghost costume
to scare trick-or-treaters

be scared by someone sitting in a tree dressed up
as a ghost every time you walk by a tree while
trick-or-treating?

Would You Rather...

Find all your candy has been unwrapped by your little brother or sister's grubby hands

be restricted by your mom and dad to eating only two pieces of candy per day?

Get driven from house to house in the car by your dad

have your mom go up to every house with you while trick-or-treating?

Would You Rather...

Go trick-or-treating dressed as an angel who gets lots of candy even though you keep stomping on little kid's toes

as a devil who has excellent manners but keeps getting less candy than everyone else?

Not be able to chew any of your Halloween candy with your teeth

eat all your Halloween candy without using your hands?

Would You Rather...

Spend your Halloween night as an ant squished
to the bottom of a trick-or-treater's shoe

as a doorbell getting touched by kids' grubby fingers?

Ding-
Dong-

Have all of your Halloween candy wrappers get stuck
to the pieces of candy so it takes you five minutes
to unwrap each piece

find that half of your pieces of candy are already
unwrapped and your parents make you throw them away?

Would You Rather...

Use your grandma's big bulky purse

OR

your grandpa's floppy grey sock as a candy bag?

Hand out candy at your house trying to keep your puppy
from running out the door every time
a trick-or-treater rings the bell

OR

find out that your puppy ate a chocolate bar and is barfing
all over the house?

Try to bite into a caramel apple when you're missing your two front teeth

try to eat a sticky popcorn ball using only your thumbs?

Get one tooth cavity in your mouth for every piece of candy you eat on Halloween

hear a voice in your head that says "I'll rot your teeth" every time you eat a piece of candy on Halloween?

Would You Rather...

Suck the sugar out of your Halloween candy
with vampire fangs

eat your candy with werewolf hands that get
fur stuck on all the candy?

Have to take your younger brother or sister
trick-or-treating and wear a matching costume

go to a Halloween party with your mom or dad
wearing a matching costume?

Would You Rather...

Eat the raw stringy guts of a jack-o-lantern

eat one pound of candy corns in ten minutes?

Hand out Halloween candy at your house and every kid that comes to your door squirts you with water

go trick-or-treating but trip and fall every time you get to someone's doorstep?

Have to babysit a really naughty little kid all night and earn $50,

get to go trick-or-treating as long as you want and have a pillowcase full of candy?

Go trick-or-treating wearing a full snowsuit under your costume

wear a skimpy costume trick-or-treating on a chilly night with no jacket on?

Trip and fall down the sidewalk while trick-or-treating and bloody your knees really bad

eat too much Halloween candy and throw up for an hour straight?

Gain five pounds on only your hands

only your feet from all of the Halloween candy you eat?

Lose six of your teeth when they get stuck
in a popcorn ball

wear shoes that are filled with melted caramel?

Stay at home all Halloween night and have to hand out
candy but get to eat however many pieces you want

go trick-or-treating for as long as you want but only
get to eat five pieces of candy all night?

Would You Rather...

Only ride on a splintery witch's broom
trick-or-treating on Halloween

trick-or-treat with the body of a zombie
you can't control?

Have a hole in the bottom of your trick-or-treating bag
that drops out pieces of candy and not know it

find lots of random stepped-on pieces of candy on the
sidewalk while you trick-or-treat?

Would You Rather...

Find a giant hard shelled six-legged beetle crawling
in your Halloween bag

bite into a piece of candy that has a tiny crunchy
bug in the middle?

Eat a giant pillowcase full of Halloween candy
in one day but not be allowed any candy
any other day of the year

only be allowed to eat one piece a day
all year long?

Get one year older for every piece
of Halloween candy you eat

get one year younger until you are wearing diapers
for every piece of Halloween candy you eat?

Have all of the Halloween candy in your
trick-or-treat bag melt into one giant ball of candy

have every piece of candy dry out, get super crumbly,
and turn to dust in your hands?

Throw up in your trick-or-treat bag

drop your bag onto a pile of still-warm dog poop?

Bite into a chocolate bar and only be able
to taste smoky-sweet baked beans

chew on a piece of gum that first tastes like
moldy bread and then like dirt?

Would You Rather...

Spill a big glass of bright red fruit punch down
the front of your costume

walk around the whole party with melted chocolate
smeared on your face and no one tells you?

Never be able to wipe off sticky candied
apple caramel

gooey melted candy-bar chocolate from
your fingers?

Would you Rather...

Try to suck a worm all the way through
a drinking straw

play pin the tail on the donkey by shooting boogers
out of your nose?

Eat cobweb flavored candy corns by picking
them off a spider web

mummy-wrapped flavored bubble gum that tastes
like it's straight from ancient Egypt?

Have to go trick-or-treating with your ankle tied
to a friend's ankle

go trick-or-treating and have to hold your mom's
hand the whole time?

Find a bunch of chewed fingernails
in your Halloween bag

find some green rubbery boogers floating
in your cup of apple juice?

Find a human eyeball in your Halloween bag

find someone's fingernail stuck to your caramel apple?

Go to a costume party at the wrong house but not realize your friends aren't there because everyone's wearing a mask

show up at a Halloween party in costume when it's not actually a costume party?

Bob for apples in a tub of squishy
old zombie brains

have a zombie with no teeth keep trying
to bite your hands?

Sneak a bunch of candy to school in your backpack
only to have it stolen

have a class Halloween party with only "healthy"
snacks like grapes and cheese sticks?

Would You Rather...

Eat too much candy at the party and have
a really bad stomachache so you can't play any games

drink too much soda and get a ridiculous case
of loud never-ending burps?

Have the day after every Halloween
as a school holiday

go to school on Halloween but get to party
all day long, with no learning activities at all?

Realize that everyone at the Halloween party is a real monster and that they are not wearing costumes

turn into a real monster on Halloween and go to a party pretending you are wearing a costume?

Play hide-and-seek in a haunted house with ghosts

play tag with a bunch of brainless zombies?

Get a ride to school on the back of
a big hairy spider

on the wings of a bumbling blind bat?

Go to a really lame Halloween party with games like
Ring Around the Pumpkin

go to a really scary Halloween party where you feel like
you're going to wet your pants because
you're so scared?

Vomit green slime every time you laugh

shoot dusty cobwebs out of your nose
every time you sneeze?

Have to finish eating a caramel apple that fell
on the floor and is covered in cat hair

have to finish eating a caramel apple that your dog
bit into and drooled all over?

Would You Rather...

Have all your teeth turn black and fall out of your mouth one day

lose one toenail per day until they are all gone?

Eat a rotten apple covered with yummy caramel

eat a pumpkin pie made from a moldy jack-o-lantern?

Catch black flies with your tongue flicking
out like a frog

swat big juicy flies with your bare hands?

Pull out some awesome dance moves at the party while
wearing a masked costume so no one knows who you are

OR

do what you think are awesome dance moves
at the party but which are really super dorky
and everyone is watching you?

Have your dog bring you a human bone it dug
up in your backyard

find out that the stray cat you found belongs to the old
witch who lives down the street and she's not happy that
you have her cat?

Have candy corn flavored ear wax

have pumpkin spice flavored boogers?

Have it rain your favorite melt-in-your-mouth chocolate bars

your favorite can't-chew-enough bubble gum?

Go to a Halloween party and change costumes every ten minutes, so no one ever knows who you are

go to a Halloween party not wearing any pants and not realize it?

Would You Rather...

Always hear a creepy scratching sound coming from your computer

always have the feeling that someone is following you?

Go through a haunted house filled with clowns so scary you can never again go to the circus

go through a haunted house filled with dolls so creepy that you can't go down your favorite store's toy aisle anymore?

Would You Rather...

Have a really hungry monster as your babysitter
and he always eats all of your supper

a giant slug as a pet that leaves slime trails all over
everything in your house?

Eat so much candy on Halloween that you go into a sugar
coma and oversleep for school the next morning

drink a big glass of ooey gooey melted caramel
for breakfast?

Would You Rather...

Take a bath in a tub full of apple juice made from squishy rotten apples

be stuck inside a giant rotten apple and have to eat your way out?

Watch a scary movie with your friends that makes you pee your pants a little

be so scared while watching the movie that you can't stop laughing and your friends get really mad at you?

Would You Rather...

Eat a donut covered with moldy cheese that you thought was frosting

eat a bunch of orange cobwebs that you thought was cotton candy?

Rather have pinky fingers that are twice as long as the rest of your fingers

have big toes that are the size of your pointer fingers?

Would You Rather...

Sit at a school desk made from an old dusty coffin
that creaks at you

be taught by a teacher who is a ghost like Professor Binns
in the Harry Potter books?

Get halfway across the playground monkey bars
and find a big spider climbing across

get halfway down the slide and realize there
are a bunch of snakes waiting at the end?

Have a best friend who is a ghost and
no one else can see

a teacher who is secretly a purple monster
with one giant eye and six tentacles that
only you can see?

Be chased by a werewolf with a doll's head
on its body

be chased by a bunch of baby dolls who are missing
random body parts?

Would You Rather...

Win a contest by smashing as many
jack-o-lanterns as you can with your bare feet

by stacking as many jack-o-lanterns as you can
on top of your head?

Your scaredy-cat scream sounds like
a cow mooing

nails on a chalkboard while going through
a haunted house?

Would You Rather...

Get lost and left to wander alone all night
in a corn maze with creepy sounds all around you

accidentally get locked overnight in your school
and hear spooky rattling sounds from
all of the hallways?

Laugh silently every time something you
hear is funny

scream like you are underwater at the pool every time
something you see is scary?

Would You Rather...

Grow devil horns out of your head every time
you think a mean thought

grow a green wart on your nose every time
you take a shower?

See scary haired clowns with big eyes wherever
you go on Halloween

sleep in a room with one hundred clown dolls?

Would You Rather...

Walk barefoot through a floor covered in smashed pumpkin guts

have a food fight in the cafeteria using raw pumpkin guts?

Hear the sound of beetles crunching every step that you take

the sound of worms squishing every step that you take?

Would You Rather...

Freak out in a haunted house and run around like a crazy person screaming "Let me out of here!"

go through a haunted house for thirty minutes and not get scared even once?

Eat a mud patty squished in between two hamburger buns

a slimy pickled earthworm?

Would you Rather...

Sleep like a bat hanging upside down from your ceiling
with your wings wrapped around your body

sleep like a wolfman in the doghouse all alone
on a chilly fall night?

Be chased around the playground by an enormous
eight-legged hairy spider

have a slide race with a really big muddy earthworm?

Would You Rather...

Carve a pumpkin using only your super sharp really long fingernails

carve a pumpkin using super-hot laser beams shot from your eyes?

Have a classmate who says "Howloween" and howls every single time she hears the word Halloween

have a classmate who spends the whole Halloween day trying to scare you by hiding and screaming "Boo!" wherever you go?

Howl out your window to the moon
at midnight every night

cackle while you cook a witch's brew for
supper every night?

Grow vampire claws that you have to trim with
a weed whacker

werewolf fur that needs to be mowed with
a lawnmower?

Would You Rather...

Have to take a really important test at school after having your brain eaten by zombies the night before

after spending all night in a haunted house and not getting any sleep at all?

Rather carve a jack-o-lantern using only your toes

with one hand tied behind your back?

Would You Rather...

Eat a hamburger that looks like it's
dripping in blood

a chicken nugget that is covered in bird feathers?

Your dad is hairy like a werewolf but also like a princess
so you always have to braid his hair

your mom is wrinkly like an old crusty mummy and she
needs you to apply lotion to her body twice a day?

Would you Rather...

Drink an earthworm smoothie made with dirt from the cemetery

eat a bowlful of green jello made from boogers?

Play a game of basketball against a team of zombies who keep trying to eat the ball

play baseball with a team of zombies whose arms keep falling off?

Get trapped in a giant sticky spider web

in a vampire's coffin on Halloween night?

Eat a bunch of Halloween chocolates that smell like toe
cheese but melt in your mouth

eat a bunch of Halloween taffy that looks like toe cheese
but tastes like fruit punch?

Wake up and find a bunch of spiders crawling
around in your hair

go to school and have spiders randomly crawling out
of your ears all day?

Only be able to scream out of your belly button

cry out of your armpits when you're scared?

Would You Rather...

Have a mysterious third hand that does things like feed you while you're working on homework

have a mysterious third eye that can see ghosts walking around?

Be frightened at the last minute before you fall asleep at night

very first thing when you wake up in the morning?

Would You Rather...

Have the face of a jack-o-lantern that always looks happy when you're sad

the face of a jack-o-lantern that always looks scary and mad when you're happy?

Scream every time you hear the word "boo"

cry every time you say the words "trick or treat"?

Have your birthday on Halloween and only
get candy for presents

have your birthday on Christmas and only
get cookies for presents?

Drink a cup of witch's brew that makes you look beautiful
when you look in the mirror but ugly to everyone else

one that makes you beautiful to everyone else
but ugly when you look in the mirror?

Be a superhero with a rocket-powered tricycle

a leap-buildings-in-a-single-bound pogo stick?

Have a pet spider who can do your homework eight times as fast as you can because of his eight arms

be an alien's pet human and have to clean up his slime-covered spaceship?

Would You Rather...

Your grandpa is a secret vampire who sleeps
in a coffin and drinks blood

your grandma is a secret witch who has
a creepy gray cat and boils things like eyeballs?

Hear the sound of creepy rattling bones

have your room fill with a thick scary fog every night
when you lay down in bed?

Would You Rather...

Wear a sock full of creepy crawly spiders

a hat full of crunchy cockroaches?

Sleep overnight in an empty grave covered with dirt

walk through a graveyard with scary hands clawing
their way out of graves?

Would You Rather...

Read a book that keeps mysteriously turning
the pages before you're ready

write with a pencil that randomly makes squiggles
all over the paper?

Be afraid of the dark and trapped
in an abandoned cemetery

be afraid of clowns and trapped
in the middle of a circus?

Find your jack-o-lantern in a different place
each morning and no one is moving it

wake up to find your jack-o-lantern sleeping
in bed next to you?

Sleep inside a cobweb-covered coffin
like Dracula

take a bath in a tub full of sloshy green slime?

Have a mouthful of candy corns instead of teeth

have a big slimy worm instead of a tongue?

Sleep overnight in a toy store filled with creepy dolls that come alive at night and all want to be your best friend

wake up in the morning and have been turned into a real life doll with rosy red cheeks and fake curly blond hair?

Eat a bowlful of spaghetti that looks like zombie brains

eat a bunch of grapes that look like slimy eyeballs?

Get caught by your school Principal while trying to toilet paper her house on Halloween

accidently step in a bunch of stinky rotten eggs someone was using as a prank on Halloween?

Would you Rather...

Leave spots of fuzzy green mold
on everything you touch

find spots of fuzzy green mold on everything
you get at the school cafeteria?

Never be able to get the taste of dirt out
of your mouth

never be able to smell anything except
moldy bread?

Did You Enjoy The Book ?

If you did, we are ecstatic. If not, please write your complaint to us and we will ensure we fix it.

If you're feeling generous, there is something important that you can help me with – tell other people that you enjoyed the book.

Ask a grown-up to write about it on Amazon. When they do, more people will find out about the book. It also lets Amazon know that we are making kids around the world enjoy reading and asking and answering 'Would you rather ...' questions. Even a few words and ratings would go a long way.

If you have any ideas or Would you rather ... questions that you think are interesting, please let us know. We would love to hear from you.

Our email address is -
riddleland@riddlelandforkids.com

109

Riddleland Bonus

Join our **Facebook Group** at **Riddleland for Kids**
to get daily jokes and riddles.

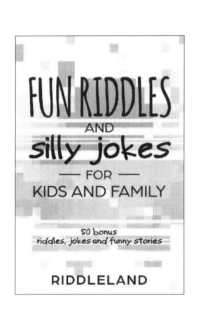

https://pixelfy.me/riddlelandbonus

Thank you for buying this book. As a token of our appreciation,
we would like to offer a special bonus—a collection of
50 original jokes, riddles, and funny stories.

CONTEST

Would you like your jokes and riddles to be featured in our next book?

We are having a contest to see who are the smartest or funniest boys and girls in the world!

1) Creative and Challenging Riddles
2) Tickle Your Funny Bone Contest

Parents, please email us your child's "original" riddle or joke. He or she could win a Riddleland book and be featured in our next book.

Here are the rules:

1) It must be challenging for the riddles and funny for the jokes!

2) It must be 100% original and not something from the Internet! It is easy to find out!

3) You can submit both jokes and riddles as they are 2 separate contests.

4) No help from the parents unless they are as funny as you.

5) Winners will be announced via email or our Facebook group - Riddleland for kids

6) Please also mention what book you purchased.

Email us at **Riddleland@riddlelandforkids.com**

111

Other Fun Books by Riddleland
Riddles Series

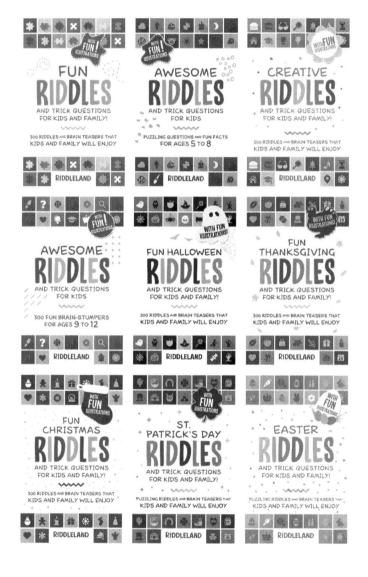

Would You Rather Questions ?

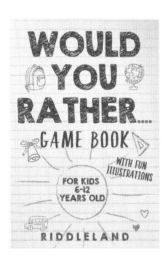 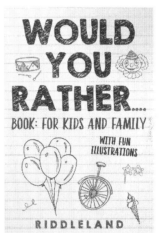

Get them on Amazon or our website at
www.riddlelandforkids.com

ABOUT RIDDLELAND

Riddleland is a mom + dad run publishing company. We are passionate about creating fun and innovative books to help children develop their reading skills and fall in love with reading. If you have suggestions for us or want to work with us, shoot us an email at

riddleland@riddlelandforkids.com

Our favorite family quote

"Creativity is an area in which younger people have a tremendous advantage since they have an endearing habit of always questioning past wisdom and authority."

– Bill Hewlett

114

84178532R00063